The Gardener

The Gardener

Rabindranath Tagore

MINT EDITIONS

The Gardener was first published in 1913.

This edition published by Mint Editions 2021.

ISBN 9781513215914 | E-ISBN 9781513213910

Published by Mint Editions®

**MINT
EDITIONS**

minteditionbooks.com

Publishing Director: Jennifer Newens
Design & Production: Rachel Lopez Metzger
Project Manager: Micaela Clark
Translated by: Rabindranath Tagore from the original Bengali
Typesetting: Westchester Publishing Services

Contents

19	29
20	30
21	31
22	32
23	33
24	34
25	35
26	36
27	37
28	38
29	39
30	40
31	41
32	42
33	43
34	44
35	45
36	46
37	47
38	48

39	49
40	50
41	51
42	52
43	53
44	54
45	55
46	56
47	57
48	58
49	59
50	60
51	61
52	62
53	63
54	64
55	65
56	66
57	67
58	68

79

80

81

82

83

84

85

90

91

92

93

94

95

96

1

SERVANT: Have mercy upon your servant, my queen!

QUEEN: The assembly is over and my servants are all gone. Why do you come at this late hour?

SERVANT: When you have finished with others, that is my time.

I come to ask what remains for your last servant to do.

QUEEN: What can you expect when it is too late?

SERVANT: Make me the gardener of your flower garden.

QUEEN: What folly is this?

SERVANT: I will give up my other work.

I will throw my swords and lances down in the dust. Do not send me to distant courts; do not bid me undertake new conquests. But make me the gardener of your flower garden.

QUEEN: What will your duties be?

SERVANT: The service of your idle days.

I will keep fresh the grassy path where you walk in the morning, where your feet will be greeted with praise at every step by the flowers eager for death.

I will swing you in a swing among the branches of the *saptaparna*, where the early evening moon will struggle to kiss your skirt through the leaves.

I will replenish with scented oil the lamp that burns by your bedside, and decorate your footstool with sandal and saffron paste in wondrous designs.

QUEEN: What will you have for your reward?

SERVANT: To be allowed to hold your little fists like tender lotus-buds and slip flower chains over your wrists; to tinge the soles of your feet with the red juice of *ashoka* petals and kiss away the speck of dust that may chance to linger there.

QUEEN: Your prayers are granted, my servant, you will be the gardener of my flower garden.

2

"Ah, poet, the evening draws near; your hair is turning grey.
"Do you in your lonely musing hear the message of the hereafter?"

"It is evening," the poet said, "and I am listening because someone may
    call from the village, late though it be.
"I watch if young straying hearts meet together, and two pairs of eager
    eyes beg for music to break their silence and speak for them.
"Who is there to weave their passionate songs, if I sit on the shore of
    life and contemplate death and the beyond?

"The early evening star disappears.
"The glow of a funeral pyre slowly dies by the silent river.
"Jackals cry in chorus from the courtyard of the deserted house in the
    light of the worn-out moon.
"If some wanderer, leaving home, come here to watch the night and
    with bowed head listen to the murmur of the darkness, who is
    there to whisper the secrets of life into his ears if I, shutting my
    doors, should try to free myself from mortal bonds?

"It is a trifle that my hair is turning grey.
"I am ever as young or as old as the youngest and the oldest of this
    village.
"Some have smiles, sweet and simple, and some a sly twinkle in their
    eyes.
"Some have tears that well up in the daylight, and others tears that are
    hidden in the gloom.
They all have need for me, and I have no time to brood over the
    afterlife.
"I am of an age with each, what matter if my hair turns grey?"

3

In the morning I cast my net into the sea.

I dragged up from the dark abyss things of strange aspect and strange beauty—some shone like a smile, some glistened like tears, and some were flushed like the cheeks of a bride.

When with the day's burden I went home, my love was sitting in the garden idly tearing the leaves of a flower.

I hesitated for a moment, and then placed at her feet all that I had dragged up, and stood silent.

She glanced at them and said, "What strange things are these? I know not of what use they are!"

I bowed my head in shame and thought, "I have not fought for these, I did not buy them in the market; they are not fit gifts for her."

Then the whole night through I flung them one by one into the street.

In the morning travellers came; they picked them up and carried them into far countries.

Ah me, why did they build my house by the road to the market town?
They moor their laden boats near my trees.
They come and go and wander at their will.
I sit and watch them; my time wears on.
Turn them away I cannot. And thus my days pass by.

Night and day their steps sound by my door.
Vainly I cry, "I do not know you."
Some of them are known to my fingers, some to my nostrils, the
blood in my veins seems to know them, and some are known to my
dreams.
Turn them away I cannot. I call them and say, "Come to my house
whoever chooses. Yes, come."

In the morning the bell rings in the temple.
They come with their baskets in their hands.
Their feet are rosy red. The early light of dawn is on their faces.
Turn them away I cannot. I call them and I say, "Come to my garden
to gather flowers. Come hither."

In the mid-day the gong sounds at the palace gate.
I know not why they leave their work and linger near my hedge.
The flowers in their hair are pale and faded; the notes are languid in
their flutes.
Turn them away I cannot. I call them and say, "The shade is cool
under my trees. Come, friends."

At night the crickets chirp in the woods.
Who is it that comes slowly to my door and gently knocks?
I vaguely see the face, not a word is spoken, the stillness of the sky is
all around.
Turn away my silent guest I cannot. I look at the face through the
dark, and hours of dreams pass by.

5

I am restless. I am athirst for far-away things.
My soul goes out in a longing to touch the skirt of the dim distance.
O Great Beyond, O the keen call of thy flute!
I forget, I ever forget, that I have no wings to fly, that I am bound in
 this spot evermore.

I am eager and wakeful, I am a stranger in a strange land.
Thy breath comes to me whispering an impossible hope.
Thy tongue is known to my heart as its very own.
O Far-to-seek, O the keen call of thy flute!
I forget, I ever forget, that I know not the way, that I have not the
 winged horse.

I am listless, I am a wanderer in my heart.
In the sunny haze of the languid hours, what vast vision of thine takes
 shape in the blue of the sky!
O Farthest end, O the keen call of thy flute!
I forget, I ever forget, that the gates are shut everywhere in the house
 where I dwell alone!

6

The tame bird was in a cage, the free bird was in the forest.
They met when the time came, it was a decree of fate.
The free bird cries, "O my love, let us fly to wood."
The cage bird whispers, "Come hither, let us both live in the cage."
Says the free bird, "Among bars, where is there room to spread one's wings?"
"Alas," cries the cage bird, "I should not know where to sit perched in the sky."

The free bird cries, "My darling, sing the songs of the woodlands."
The cage bird says, "Sit by my side, I'll teach you the speech of the learned."
The forest bird cries, "No, ah no! songs can never be taught."
The cage bird says, "Alas for me, I know not the songs of the woodlands."

Their love is intense with longing, but they never can fly wing to wing.
Through the bars of the cage they look, and vain is their wish to know each other.
They flutter their wings in yearning, and sing, "Come closer, my love!"
The free bird cries, "It cannot be, I fear the closed doors of the cage."
The cage bird whispers, "Alas, my wings are powerless and dead."

O mother, the young Prince is to pass by our door,—how can I attend
to my work this morning?
Show me how to braid up my hair; tell me what garment to put on.
Why do you look at me amazed, mother?
I know well he will not glance up once at my window; I know he will
pass out of my sight in the twinkling of an eye; only the vanishing
strain of the flute will come sobbing to me from afar.
But the young Prince will pass by our door, and I will put on my best
for the moment.

O mother, the young Prince did pass by our door, and the morning
sun flashed from his chariot.
I swept aside the veil from my face, I tore the ruby chain from my
neck and flung it in his path.
Why do you look at me amazed, mother?
I know well he did not pick up my chain; I know it was crushed under
his wheels leaving a red stain upon the dust, and no one knows
what my gift was nor to whom.
But the young Prince did pass by our door, and I flung the jewel from
my breast before his path.

8

When the lamp went out by my bed I woke up with the early birds.
I sat at my open window with a fresh wreath on my loose hair.
The young traveller came along the road in the rosy mist of the
    morning.
A pearl chain was on his neck, and the sun's rays fell on his crown. He
    stopped before my door and asked me with an eager cry, "Where
    is she?"
For very shame I could not say, "She is I, young traveller, she is I."

It was dusk and the lamp was not lit.
I was listlessly braiding my hair.
The young traveller came on his chariot in the glow of the setting sun.
His horses were foaming at the mouth, and there was dust on his
    garment.
He alighted at my door and asked in a tired voice, "Where is she?"
For very shame I could not say, "She is I, weary traveller, she is I."

It is an April night. The lamp is burning in my room.
The breeze of the south comes gently. The noisy parrot sleeps in its
    cage.
My bodice is of the colour of the peacock's throat, and my mantle is
    green as young grass.
I sit upon the floor at the window watching the deserted street.
Through the dark night I keep humming, "She is I, despairing traveller,
    she is I."

When I go alone at night to my love-tryst, birds do not sing, the wind
does not stir, the houses on both sides of the street stand silent.
It is my own anklets that grow loud at every step and I am ashamed.

When I sit on my balcony and listen for his footsteps, leaves do not
rustle on the trees, and the water is still in the river like the sword
on the knees of a sentry fallen asleep.
It is my own heart that beats wildly—I do not know how to quiet it.

When my love comes and sits by my side, when my body trembles and
my eyelids droop, the night darkens, the wind blows out the lamp,
and the clouds draw veils over the stars.
It is the jewel at my own breast that shines and gives light. I do not
know how to hide it.

Let your work be, bride. Listen, the guest has come.
Do you hear, he is gently shaking the chain which fastens the door?
See that your anklets make no loud noise, and that your step is not
    over-hurried at meeting him.
Let your work be, bride, the guest has come in the evening.

No, it is not the ghostly wind, bride, do not be frightened.
It is the full moon on a night of April; shadows are pale in the
    courtyard; the sky overhead is bright.
Draw your veil over your face if you must, carry the lamp to the door
    if you fear.
No, it is not the ghostly wind, bride, do not be frightened.

Have no word with him if you are shy; stand aside by the door when
    you meet him.
If he asks you questions, and if you wish to, you can lower your eyes in
    silence.
Do not let your bracelets jingle when, lamp in hand, you lead him in.
Have no word with him if you are shy.

Have you not finished your work yet, bride? Listen, the guest has
    come.
Have you not lit the lamp in the cowshed?
Have you not got ready the offering basket for the evening service?
Have you not put the red lucky mark at the parting of your hair, and
    done your toilet for the night?
O bride, do you hear, the guest has come?
Let your work be!

11

Come as you are; do not loiter over your toilet.
If your braided hair has loosened, if the parting of your hair be not
   straight, if the ribbons of your bodice be not fastened, do not mind.
Come as you are; do not loiter over your toilet.

Come, with quick steps over the grass.
If the raddle come from your feet because of the dew, if the rings of
   bells upon your feet slacken, if pearls drop out of your chain, do
   not mind.
Come with quick steps over the grass.

Do you see the clouds wrapping the sky?
Flocks of cranes fly up from the further river-bank and fitful gusts of
   wind rush over the heath.
The anxious cattle run to their stalls in the village.
Do you see the clouds wrapping the sky?

In vain you light your toilet lamp—it flickers and goes out in the wind.
Who can know that your eyelids have not been touched with lamp-
   black? For your eyes are darker than rain-clouds.
In vain you light your toilet lamp—it goes out.

Come as you are; do not loiter over your toilet.
If the wreath is not woven, who cares; if the wrist-chain has not been
   linked, let it be.
The sky is overcast with clouds—it is late.
Come as you are; do not loiter over your toilet.

If you would be busy and fill your pitcher, come, O come to my lake.
The water will cling round your feet and babble its secret.
The shadow of the coming rain is on the sands, and the clouds hang
    low upon the blue lines of the trees like the heavy hair above your
    eyebrows.
I know well the rhythm of your steps, they are beating in my heart.
Come, O come to my lake, if you must fill your pitcher.

If you would be idle and sit listless and let your pitcher float on the
    water, come, O come to my lake.
The grassy slope is green, and the wild flowers beyond number.
Your thoughts will stray out of your dark eyes like birds from their
    nests.
Your veil will drop to your feet.
Come, O come to my lake if you must sit idle.

If you would leave off your play and dive in the water, come, O come
    to my lake.
Let your blue mantle lie on the shore; the blue water will cover you
    and hide you.
The waves will stand a-tiptoe to kiss your neck and whisper in your
    ears.
Come, O come to my lake, if you would dive in the water.

If you must be mad and leap to your death, come, O come to my lake.
It is cool and fathomlessly deep.
It is dark like a sleep that is dreamless.
There in its depths nights and days are one, and songs are silence.
Come, O come to my lake, if you would plunge to your death.

13

I asked nothing, only stood at the edge of the wood behind the tree.
Languor was still upon the eyes of the dawn, and the dew in the air.
The lazy smell of the damp grass hung in the thin mist above the earth.
Under the banyan tree you were milking the cow with your hands,
    tender and fresh as butter.
And I was standing still.

I did not say a word. It was the bird that sang unseen from the thicket.
The mango tree was shedding its flowers upon the village road, and
    the bees came humming one by one.
On the side of the pond the gate of *Shiva's* temple was opened and the
    worshipper had begun his chants.
With the vessel on your lap you were milking the cow.
I stood with my empty can.

I did not come near you.
The sky woke with the sound of the gong at the temple.
The dust was raised in the road from the hoofs of the driven cattle.
With the gurgling pitchers at their hips, women came from the river.
Your bracelets were jingling, and foam brimming over the jar.
The morning wore on and I did not come near you.

14

I was walking by the road, I do not know why, when the noonday was
past and bamboo branches rustled in the wind.
The prone shadows with their out-stretched arms clung to the feet of
the hurrying light.
The *koels* were weary of their songs.
I was walking by the road, I do not know why.

The hut by the side of the water is shaded by an overhanging tree.
Someone was busy with her work, and her bangles made music in the
corner.
I stood before this hut, I know not why.

The narrow winding road crosses many a mustard field, and many a
mango forest.
It passes by the temple of the village and the market at the river
landing place.
I stopped by this hut, I do not know why.

Years ago it was a day of breezy March when the murmur of the spring
was languorous, and mango blossoms were dropping on the dust.
The rippling water leapt and licked the brass vessel that stood on the
landing step.
I think of that day of breezy March, I do not know why.

Shadows are deepening and cattle returning to their folds.
The light is grey upon the lonely meadows, and the villagers are
waiting for the ferry at the bank.
I slowly return upon my steps, I do not know why.

I run as a musk-deer runs in the shadow of the forest mad with his
    own perfume.
The night is the night of mid-May, the breeze is the breeze of the
    south.
I lose my way and I wander, I seek what I cannot get, I get what I do
    not seek.

From my heart comes out and dances the image of my own desire.
The gleaming vision flits on.
I try to clasp it firmly, it eludes me and leads me astray.
I seek what I cannot get, I get what I do not seek.

16

Hands cling to hands and eyes linger on eyes: thus begins the record of our hearts.

It is the moonlit night of March; the sweet smell of *henna* is in the air; my flute lies on the earth neglected and your garland of flowers in unfinished.

This love between you and me is simple as a song.

Your veil of the saffron colour makes my eyes drunk.

The jasmine wreath that you wove me thrills to my heart like praise.

It is a game of giving and withholding, revealing and screening again; some smiles and some little shyness, and some sweet useless struggles.

This love between you and me is simple as a song.

No mystery beyond the present; no striving for the impossible; no shadow behind the charm; no groping in the depth of the dark.

This love between you and me is simple as a song.

We do not stray out of all words into the ever silent; we do not raise our hands to the void for things beyond hope.

It is enough what we give and we get.

We have not crushed the joy to the utmost to wring from it the wine of pain.

This love between you and me is simple as a song.

The yellow bird sings in their tree and makes my heart dance with
    gladness.
We both live in the same village, and that is our one piece of joy.
Her pair of pet lambs come to graze in the shade of our garden trees.
If they stray into our barley field, I take them up in my arms.
The name of our village is Khanjan, and Anjan they call our river.
My name is known to all the village, and her name is Ranjan.

Only one field lies between us.
Bees that have hived in our grove go to seek honey in theirs.
Flowers launched from their landing-stairs come floating by the
    stream where we bathe.
Baskets of dried *kusm* flowers come from their fields to our market.
The name of our village is Khanjan, and Anjan they call our river.
My name is known to all the village, and her name is Ranjan.

The lane that winds to their house is fragrant in the spring with
    mango flowers.
When their linseed is ripe for harvest the hemp is in bloom in our
    field.
The stars that smile on their cottage send us the same twinkling look.
The rain that floods their tank makes glad our *kadam* forest.
The name of our village is Khanjan, and Anjan they call our river.
My name is known to all the village, and her name is Ranjan.

18

When the two sisters go to fetch water, they come to this spot and
they smile.
They must be aware of somebody who stands behind the trees
whenever they go to fetch water.

The two sisters whisper to each other when they pass this spot.
They must have guessed the secret of that somebody who stands
behind the trees whenever they go to fetch water.
Their pitchers lurch suddenly, and water spills when they reach this
spot.
They must have found out that somebody's heart is beating who stands
behind the trees whenever they go to fetch water.

The two sisters glance at each other when they come to this spot, and
they smile.
There is a laughter in their swift-stepping feet, which makes confusion
in somebody's mind who stands behind the trees whenever they go
to fetch water.

You walked by the riverside path with the full pitcher upon your hip.

Why did you swiftly turn your face and peep at me through your fluttering veil?

That gleaming look from the dark came upon me like a breeze that sends a shiver through the rippling water and sweeps away to the shadowy shore.

It came to me like the bird of the evening that hurriedly flies across the lampless room from the one open window to the other, and disappears in the night.

You are hidden as a star behind the hills, and I am a passer-by upon the road.

But why did you stop for a moment and glance at my face through your veil while you walked by the riverside path with the full pitcher upon your hip?

Day after day he comes and goes away.
Go, and give him a flower from my hair, my friend.
If he asks who was it that sent it, I entreat you do not tell him my
    name—for he only comes and goes away.

He sits on the dust under the tree.
Spread there a seat with flowers and leaves, my friend.
His eyes are sad, and they bring sadness to my heart.
He does not speak what he has in mind; he only comes and goes away.

21

Why did he choose to come to my door, the wandering youth, when
the day dawned?
As I come in and out I pass by him everytime, and my eyes are caught
by his face.
I know not if I should speak to him or keep silent. Why did he choose
to come to my door?

The cloudy nights in July are dark; the sky is soft blue in the autumn;
the spring days are restless with the south wind.
He weaves his songs with fresh tunes everytime.
I turn from my work and my eyes fill with the mist. Why did he
choose to come to my door?

22

When she passed by me with quick steps, the end of her skirt
touched me.

From the unknown island of a heart came a sudden warm breath of
spring.

A flutter of a flitting touch brushed me and vanished in a moment,
like a torn flower petal blown in the breeze.

It fell upon my heart like a sigh of her body and whisper of her heart.

23

Why do you sit there and jingle your bracelets in mere idle sport?
Fill your pitcher. It is time for you to come home.

Why do you stir the water with your hands and fitfully glance at the
   road for someone in mere idle sport?
Fill your pitcher and come home.

The morning hours pass by—the dark water flows on.
The waves are laughing and whispering to each other in mere idle
   sport.

The wandering clouds have gathered at the edge of the sky on yonder
   rise of the land.
They linger and look at your face and smile in mere idle sport.
Fill your pitcher and come home.

Do not keep to yourself the secret of your heart, my friend!
Say it to me, only to me, in secret.
You who smile so gently, softly whisper, my heart will hear it, not
my ears.

The night is deep, the house is silent, the birds' nests are shrouded
with sleep.
Speak to me through hesitating tears, through faltering smiles,
through sweet shame and pain, the secret of your heart!

"Come to us, youth, tell us truly why there is madness in your eyes?"
"I know not what wine of wild poppy I have drunk, that there is this
madness in my eyes."
"Ah, shame!"
"Well, some are wise and some foolish, some are watchful and some
careless. There are eyes that smile and eyes that weep—and
madness is in my eyes."

"Youth, why do you stand so still under the shadow of the tree?"
"My feet are languid with the burden of my heart, and I stand still in
the shadow."
"Ah, shame!"
"Well, some march on their way and some linger, some are free and
some are fettered—and my feet are languid with the burden of
my heart."

"What comes from your willing hands I take. I beg for nothing more."
"Yes, yes, I know you, modest mendicant, you ask for all that one has."

"If there be a stray flower for me I will wear it in my heart."
"But if there be thorns?"
"I will endure them."
"Yes, yes, I know you, modest mendicant, you ask for all that one has."

"If but once you should raise your loving eyes to my face it would make
my life sweet beyond death."
"But if there by only cruel glances?"
"I will keep them piercing my heart."
"Yes, yes, I know you, modest mendicant, you ask for all that one has."

27

"Trust love even if it brings sorrow. Do not close up your heart."
"Ah no, my friend, your words are dark, I cannot understand them."

"The heart is only for giving away with a tear and a song, my love."
"Ah no, my friend, your words are dark, I cannot understand them."

"Pleasure is frail like a dewdrop, while it laughs it dies. But sorrow is
strong and abiding. Let sorrowful love wake in your eyes."
"Ah no, my friend, your words are dark, I cannot understand them."

"The lotus blooms in the sight of the sun, and loses all that it has. It
would not remain in bud in the eternal winter mist."
"Ah no, my friend, your words are dark, I cannot understand them."

Your questioning eyes are sad. They seek to know my meaning as the
moon would fathom the sea.

I have bared my life before your eyes from end to end, with nothing
hidden or held back. That is why you know me not.

If it were only a gem I could break it into a hundred pieces and string
them into a chain to put on your neck.

If it were only a flower, round and small and sweet, I could pluck it
from its stem to set it in your hair.

But it is a heart, my beloved. Where are its shores and its bottom?

You know not the limits of this kingdom, still you are its queen.

If it were only a moment of pleasure it would flower in an easy smile,
and you could see it and read it in a moment.

If it were merely a pain it would melt in limpid tears, reflecting its
inmost secret without a word.

But it is love, my beloved.

Its pleasure and pain are boundless, and endless its wants and wealth.

It is as near to you as your life, but you can never wholly know it.

29

Speak to me, my love! Tell me in words what you sang.

The night is dark. The stars are lost in clouds. The wind is sighing through the leaves.

I will let loose my hair. My blue cloak will cling round me like night. I will clasp your head to my bosom; and there in the sweet loneliness murmur on your heart. I will shut my eyes and listen. I will not look in your face.

When your words are ended, we will sit still and silent. Only the trees will whisper in the dark.

The night will pale. The day will dawn. We shall look at each other's eyes and go on our different paths.

Speak to me, my love! Tell me in words what you sang.

30

You are the evening cloud floating in the sky of my dreams.
I paint you and fashion you ever with my love longings.
You are my own, my own, Dweller in my endless dreams!

Your feet are rosy-red with the glow of my heart's desire, Gleaner of
my sunset songs!
Your lips are bitter-sweet with the taste of my wine of pain.
You are my own, my own, Dweller in my lonesome dreams!

With the shadow of my passion have I darkened your eyes, Haunter of
the depth of my gaze!
I have caught you and wrapt you, my love, in the net of my music.
You are my own, my own, Dweller in my deathless dreams!

My heart, the bird of the wilderness, has found its sky in your eyes.
They are the cradle of the morning, they are the kingdom of the stars.
My songs are lost in their depths.
Let me but soar in that sky, in its lonely immensity.
Let me but cleave its clouds and spread wings in its sunshine.

32

Tell me if this be all true, my lover, tell me if this be true.

When these eyes flash their lightning the dark clouds in your breast
make stormy answer.

Is it true that my lips are sweet like the opening bud of the first
conscious love?

Do the memories of vanished months of May linger in my limbs?

Does the earth, like a harp, shiver into songs with the touch of my
feet?

Is it then true that the dewdrops fall from the eyes of night when I am
seen, and the morning light is glad when it wraps my body round?

Is it true, is it true, that your love travelled alone through ages and
worlds in search of me?

That when you found me at last, your age-long desire found utter
peace in my gentle speech and my eyes and lips and flowing hair?

Is it then true that the mystery of the Infinite is written on this little
forehead of mine?

Tell me, my lover, if all this be true.

33

I love you, beloved. Forgive me my love.
Like a bird losing its way I am caught.
When my heart was shaken it lost its veil and was naked. Cover it
    with pity, beloved, and forgive me my love.

If you cannot love me, beloved, forgive me my pain.
Do not look askance at me from afar.
I will steal back to my corner and sit in the dark.
With both hands I will cover my naked shame.
Turn your face from me, beloved, and forgive me my pain.

If you love me, beloved, forgive me my joy.
When my heart is borne away by the flood of happiness, do not smile
    at my perilous abandonment.
When I sit on my throne and rule you with my tyranny of love, when
    like a goddess I grant you my favour, bear with my pride, beloved,
    and forgive me my joy.

Do not go, my love, without asking my leave.
I have watched all night, and now my eyes are heavy with sleep.
I fear lest I lose you when I am sleeping.
Do not go, my love, without asking my leave.

I start up and stretch my hands to touch you. I ask myself, "Is it a
    dream?"
Could I but entangle your feet with my heart and hold them fast to
    my breast!
Do not go, my love, without asking my leave.

Lest I should know you too easily, you play with me.
You blind me with flashes of laughter to hide your tears.
I know, I know your art.
You never say the word you would.

Lest I should not prize you, you elude me in a thousand ways.
Lest I should confuse you with the crowd, you stand aside.
I know, I know your art,
You never walk the path you would.

Your claim is more than that of others, that is why you are silent.
With playful carelessness you avoid my gifts.
I know, I know your art,
You never will take what you would.

He whispered, "My love, raise your eyes."

I sharply chid him, and said "Go!"; but he did not stir.

He stood before me and held both my hands. I said, "Leave me!"; but he did not go.

He brought his face near my ear. I glanced at him and said, "What a shame!"; but he did not move.

His lips touched my cheek. I trembled and said, "You dare too much"; but he had no shame.

He put a flower in my hair. I said, "It is useless!"; but he stood unmoved.

He took the garland from my neck and went away. I weep and ask my heart, "Why does he not come back?"

37

Would you put your wreath of fresh flowers on my neck, fair one?
But you must know that the one wreath that I had woven is for
   the many, for those who are seen in glimpses, or dwell in lands
   unexplored, or live in poets' songs.

It is too late to ask my heart in return for yours.
There was a time when my life was like a bud, all its perfume was
   stored in its core.
Now it is squandered far and wide.
Who knows the enchantment that can gather and shut it up again?
My heart is not mine to give to one only, it is given to the many.

My love, once upon a time your poet launched a great epic in his mind.

Alas, I was not careful, and it struck your ringing anklets and came to grief.

It broke up into scraps of songs and lay scattered at your feet.

All my cargo of the stories of old wars was tossed by the laughing waves and soaked in tears and sank.

You must make this loss good to me, my love.

If my claims to immortal fame after death are shattered, make me immortal while I live.

And I will not mourn for my loss nor blame you.

I try to weave a wreath all the morning, but the flowers slip and they
    drop out.
You sit there watching me in secret through the corner of your prying
    eyes.
Ask those eyes, darkly planning mischief, whose fault it was.

I try to sing a song, but in vain.
A hidden smile trembles on your lips, ask of it the reason of my failure.
Let your smiling lips say on oath how my voice lost itself in silence
    like a drunken bee in the lotus.

It is evening, and the time for the flowers to close their petals.
Give me leave to sit by your side, and bid my lips to do the work that
    can be done in silence and in the dim light of stars.

An unbelieving smile flits on your eyes when I come to you to take my
leave.

I have done it so often that you think I will soon return.

To tell you the truth I have the same doubt in my mind.

For the spring days come again time after time; the full moon takes
leave and comes on another visit, the flowers come again and blush
upon their branches year after year, and it is likely that I take my
leave only to come to you again.

But keep the illusion awhile; do not send it away with ungentle haste.

When I say I leave you for all time, accept it as true, and let a mist of
tears for one moment deepen the dark rim of your eyes.

Then smile as archly as you like when I come again.

I long to speak the deepest words I have to say to you; but I dare not, for fear you should laugh.
That is why I laugh at myself and shatter my secret in jest.
I make light of my pain, afraid you should do so.

I long to tell you the truest words I have to say to you; but I dare not, being afraid that you would not believe them.
That is why I disguise them in untruth, saying the contrary of what I mean.
I make my pain appear absurd, afraid that you should do so.

I long to use the most precious words I have for you; but I dare not, fearing I should not be paid with like value.
That is why I gave you hard names and boast of my callous strength.
I hurt you, for fear you should never know any pain.

I long to sit silent by you; but I dare not lest my heart come out at my lips.
That is why I prattle and chatter lightly and hide my heart behind words.
I rudely handle my pain, for fear you should do so.

I long to go away from your side; but I dare not, for fear my cowardice should become known to you.
That is why I hold my head high and carelessly come into your presence.
Constant thrusts from your eyes keep my pain fresh forever.

O mad, superbly drunk;
If you kick open your doors and play the fool in public;
If you empty your bag in a night, and snap your fingers at prudence;
If you walk in curious paths and play with useless things;
Reck not rhyme or reason;
If unfurling your sails before the storm you snap the rudder in two,
Then I will follow you, comrade, and be drunken and go to the dogs.

I have wasted my days and nights in the company of steady wise
    neighbours.
Much knowing has turned my hair grey, and much watching has made
    my sight dim.
For years I have gathered and heaped up scraps and fragments of
    things;
Crush them and dance upon them, and scatter them all to the winds.
For I know 'tis the height of wisdom to be drunken and go to the dogs.

Let all crooked scruples vanish, let me hopelessly lose my way.
Let a gust of wild giddiness come and sweep me away from my
    anchors.
The world is peopled with worthies, and workers, useful and clever.
There are men who are easily first, and men who come decently after.
Let them be happy and prosper, and let me be foolishly futile.
For I know 'tis the end of all works to be drunken and go to the dogs.

I swear to surrender this moment all claims to the ranks of the decent.
I let go my pride of learning and judgment of right and of wrong.
I'll shatter memory's vessel, scattering the last drop of tears.
With the foam of the berry-red wine I will bathe and brighten my
    laughter.
The badge of the civil and staid I'll tear into shreds for the nonce.
I'll take the holy vow to be worthless, to be drunken and go to the
    dogs.

43

No, my friends, I shall never be an ascetic, whatever you may say.
I shall never be an ascetic if she does not take the vow with me.
It is my firm resolve that if I cannot find a shady shelter and a
  companion for my penance, I shall never turn ascetic.

No, my friends, I shall never leave my hearth and home, and retire
  into the forest solitude, if rings no merry laughter in its echoing
  shade and if the end of no saffron mantle flutters in the wind; if its
  silence is not deepened by soft whispers.
I shall never be an ascetic.

Reverend sir, forgive this pair of sinners. Spring winds today are
 blowing in wild eddies, driving dust and dead leaves away, and
 with them your lessons are all lost.
Do not say, father, that life is a vanity.
For we have made truce with death for once, and only for a few
 fragrant hours we two have been made immortal.

Even if the king's army came and fiercely fell upon us we should sadly
 shake our heads and say, Brothers, you are disturbing us. If you
 must have this noisy game, go and clatter your arms elsewhere.
 Since only for a few fleeting moments we have been made
 immortal.

If friendly people came and flocked around us, we should humbly
 bow to them and say, This extravagant good fortune is an
 embarrassment to us. Room is scarce in the infinite sky where we
 dwell. For in the springtime flowers come in crowds, and the busy
 wings of bees jostle each other. Our little heaven, where dwell only
 we two immortals, is too absurdly narrow.

45

To the guests that must go bid God's speed and brush away all traces
of their steps.

Take to your bosom with a smile what is easy and simple and near.

Today is the festival of phantoms that know not when they die.

Let your laughter be but a meaningless mirth like twinkles of light on
the ripples.

Let your life lightly dance on the edges of Time like dew on the tip of
a leaf.

Strike in chords from your harp fitful momentary rhythms.

You left me and went on your way.
I thought I should mourn for you and set your solitary image in my
    heart wrought in a golden song.
But ah, my evil fortune, time is short.

Youth wanes year after year; the spring days are fugitive; the frail
    flowers die for nothing, and the wise man warns me that life is but
    a dew-drop on the lotus leaf.
Should I neglect all this to gaze after one who has turned her back on
    me?
That would be rude and foolish, for time is short.

Then, come, my rainy nights with pattering feet; smile, my golden
    autumn; come, careless April, scattering your kisses abroad.
You come, and you, and you also!
My loves, you know we are mortals. Is it wise to break one's heart for
    the one who takes her heart away? For time is short.

It is sweet to sit in a corner to muse and write in rhymes that you are
    all my world.
It is heroic to hug one's sorrow and determine not to be consoled.
But a fresh face peeps across my door and raises its eyes to my eyes.
I cannot but wipe away my tears and change the tune of my song.
For time is short.

If you would have it so, I will end my singing.
If it sets your heart aflutter, I will take away my eyes from your face.
If it suddenly startles you in your walk, I will step aside and take
   another path.
If it confuses you in your flower-weaving, I will shun your lonely
   garden.
If it makes the water wanton and wild, I will not row my boat by your
   bank.

48

Free me from the bonds of your sweetness, my love! No more of this
    wine of kisses.
This mist of heavy incense stifles my heart.
Open the doors, make room for the morning light.
I am lost in you, wrapped in the folds of your caresses.
Free me from your spells, and give me back the manhood to offer you
    my freed heart.

49

I hold her hands and press her to my breast.
I try to fill my arms with her loveliness, to plunder her sweet smile
    with kisses, to drink her dark glances with my eyes.
Ah, but, where is it? Who can strain the blue from the sky?
I try to grasp the beauty, it eludes me, leaving only the body in my
    hands.
Baffled and weary I come back.
How can the body touch the flower which only the spirit may touch?

50

Love, my heart longs day and night for the meeting with you—for the meeting that is like all-devouring death.

Sweep me away like a storm; take everything I have; break open my sleep and plunder my dreams. Rob me of my world.

In that devastation, in the utter nakedness of spirit, let us become one in beauty.

Alas for my vain desire! Where is this hope for union except in thee, my God?

Then finish the last song and let us leave.

Forget this night when the night is no more.

Whom do I try to clasp in my arms? Dreams can never be made
captive.

My eager hands press emptiness to my heart and it bruises my breast.

52

Why did the lamp go out?
I shaded it with my cloak to save it from the wind, that is why the
lamp went out.

Why did the flower fade?
I pressed it to my heart with anxious love, that is why the flower faded.

Why did the stream dry up?
I put a dam across it to have it for my use, that is why the stream
dried up.

Why did the harp-string break?
I tried to force a note that was beyond its power, that is why the harp-
string is broken.

53

Why do you put me to shame with a look?
I have not come as a beggar.
Only for a passing hour I stood at the end of your courtyard outside
the garden hedge.
Why do you put me to shame with a look?

Not a rose did I gather from your garden, not a fruit did I pluck.
I humbly took my shelter under the wayside shade where every
strange traveller may stand.
Not a rose did I pluck.

Yes, my feet were tired, and the shower of rain come down.
The winds cried out among the swaying bamboo branches.
The clouds ran across the sky as though in the flight from defeat.
My feet were tired.

I know not what you thought of me or for whom you were waiting at
your door.
Flashes of lightning dazzled your watching eyes.
How could I know that you could see me where I stood in the dark?
I know not what you thought of me.

The day is ended, and the rain has ceased for a moment.
I leave the shadow of the tree at the end of your garden and this seat
on the grass.
It has darkened; shut your door; I go my way.
The day is ended.

54

Where do you hurry with your basket this late evening when the marketing is over?

They all have come home with their burdens; the moon peeps from above the village trees.

The echoes of the voices calling for the ferry run across the dark water to the distant swamp where wild ducks sleep.

Where do you hurry with your basket when the marketing is over?

Sleep has laid her fingers upon the eyes of the earth.

The nests of the crows have become silent, and the murmurs of the bamboo leaves are silent.

The labourers home from their fields spread their mats in the courtyards.

Where do you hurry with your basket when the marketing is over?

It was mid-day when you went away.
The sun was strong in the sky.
I had done my work and sat alone on my balcony when you went away.

Fitful gusts came winnowing through the smells of many distant fields.
The doves cooed tireless in the shade, and a bee strayed in my room
    humming the news of many distant fields.

The village slept in the noonday heat. The road lay deserted.
In sudden fits the rustling of the leaves rose and died.
I glazed at the sky and wove in the blue the letters of a name I had
    known, while the village slept in the noonday heat.

I had forgotten to braid my hair. The languid breeze played with it
    upon my cheek.
The river ran unruffled under the shady bank.
The lazy white clouds did not move.
I had forgotten to braid my hair.

It was mid-day when you went away.
The dust of the road was hot and the fields panting.
The doves cooed among the dense leaves.
I was alone in my balcony when you went away.

56

I was one among many women busy with the obscure daily tasks of
 the household.
Why did you single me out and bring me away from the cool shelter
 of our common life?

Love unexpressed in sacred. It shines like gems in the gloom of the
 hidden heart. In the light of the curious day it looks pitifully dark.
Ah, you broke through the cover of my heart and dragged my
 trembling love into the open place, destroying forever the shady
 corner where it hid its nest.

The other women are the same as ever.
No one has peeped into their inmost being, and they themselves know
 not their own secret.
Lightly they smile, and weep, chatter, and work. Daily they go to the
 temple, light their lamps, and fetch water from the river.

I hoped my love would be saved from the shivering shame of the
 shelterless, but you turn your face away.
Yes, your path lies open before you, but you have cut off my return,
 and left me stripped naked before the world with its lidless eyes
 staring night and day.

I plucked your flower, O world!
I pressed it to my heart and the thorn pricked.
When the day waned and it darkened, I found that the flower had
    faded, but the pain remained.

More flowers will come to you with perfume and pride, O world!
But my time for flower-gathering is over, and through the dark night I
    have not my rose, only the pain remains.

One morning in the flower garden a blind girl came to offer me a
    flower chain in the cover of a lotus leaf.
I put it round my neck, and tears came to my eyes.
I kissed her and said, "You are blind even as the flowers are.
You yourself know not how beautiful is your gift."

O woman, you are not merely the handiwork of God, but also of men;
    these are ever endowing you with beauty from their hearts.
Poets are weaving for you a web with threads of golden imagery;
    painters are giving your form ever new immortality.
The sea gives its pearls, the mines their gold, the summer gardens their
    flowers to deck you, to cover you, to make you more precious.
The desire of men's hearts has shed its glory over your youth.
You are one half woman and one half dream.

Amidst the rush and roar of life, O Beauty, carved in stone, you stand
  mute and still, alone and aloof.
Great Time sits enamoured at your feet and murmurs:
"Speak, speak to me, my love; speak, my bride!"
But your speech is shut up in stone, O Immovable Beauty!

Peace, my heart, let the time for the parting be sweet.
Let it not be a death but completeness.
Let love melt into memory and pain into songs.
Let the flight through the sky end in the folding of the wings over
    the nest.
Let the last touch of your hands be gentle like the flower of the night.
Stand still, O Beautiful End, for a moment, and say your last words in
    silence.
I bow to you and hold up my lamp to light you on your way.

62

In the dusky path of a dream I went to seek the love who was mine in
    a former life.

Her house stood at the end of a desolate street.
In the evening breeze her pet peacock sat drowsing on its perch, and
    the pigeons were silent in their corner.

She set her lamp down by the portal and stood before me.
She raised her large eyes to my face and mutely asked, "Are you well,
    my friend?"
I tried to answer, but our language had been lost and forgotten.

I thought and thought; our names would not come to my mind.
Tears shone in her eyes. She held up her right hand to me. I took it
    and stood silent.

Our lamp had flickered in the evening breeze and died.

Traveller, must you go?
The night is still and the darkness swoons upon the forest.
The lamps are bright in our balcony, the flowers all fresh, and the
    youthful eyes still awake.
Is the time for your parting come?
Traveller, must you go?

We have not bound your feet with our entreating arms.
Your doors are open. Your horse stands saddled at the gate.
If we have tried to bar your passage it was but with our songs.
Did we ever try to hold you back it was but with our eyes.
Traveller, we are helpless to keep you. We have only our tears.

What quenchless fire glows in your eyes?
What restless fever runs in your blood?
What call from the dark urges you?
What awful incantation have you read among the stars in the sky, that
    with a sealed secret message the night entered your heart, silent
    and strange?

If you do not care for merry meetings, if you must have peace, weary
    heart, we shall put our lamps out and silence our harps.
We shall sit still in the dark in the rustle of leaves, and the tired moon
    will shed pale rays on your window.
O traveller, what sleepless spirit has touched you from the heart of the
    mid-night?

I spent my day on the scorching hot dust of the road.
Now, in the cool of the evening, I knock at the door of the inn. It is
 deserted and in ruins.
A grim *ashath* tree spreads its hungry clutching roots through the
 gaping fissures of the walls.

Days have been when wayfarers came here to wash their weary feet.
They spread their mats in the courtyard in the dim light of the early
 moon, and sat and talked of strange lands.
They work refreshed in the morning when birds made them glad, and
 friendly flowers nodded their heads at them from the wayside.

But no lighted lamp awaited me when I came here.
The black smudges of smoke left by many a forgotten evening lamp
 stare, like blind eyes, from the wall.
Fireflies flit in the bush near the dried-up pond, and bamboo branches
 fling their shadows on the grass-grown path.
I am the guest of no one at the end of my day.
The long night is before me, and I am tired.

Is that your call again?
The evening has come. Weariness clings around me like the arms of
    entreating love.
Do you call me?

I had given all my day to you, cruel mistress, must you also rob me of
    my night?
Somewhere there is an end to everything, and the loneness of the dark
    is one's own.
Must your voice cut through it and smite me?

Has the evening no music of sleep at your gate?
Do the silent-winged stars never climb the sky above your pitiless
    tower?
Do the flowers never drop on the dust in soft death in your garden?

Must you call me, you unquiet one?
Then let the sad eyes of love vainly watch and weep.
Let the lamp burn in the lonely house.
Let the ferry-boat take the weary labourers to their home.
I leave behind my dreams and I hasten to your call.

A wandering madman was seeking the touchstone, with matted locks tawny and dust-laden, and body worn to a shadow, his lips tight-pressed, like the shut-up doors of his heart, his burning eyes like the lamp of a glow-worm seeking its mate.

Before him the endless ocean roared.

The garrulous waves ceaselessly talked of hidden treasures, mocking the ignorance that knew not their meaning.

Maybe he now had no hope remaining, yet he would not rest, for the search had become his life,—

Just as the ocean forever lifts its arms to the sky for the unattainable—

Just as the stars go in circles, yet seeking a goal that can never be reached—

Even so on the lonely shore the madman with dusty tawny locks still roamed in search of the touchstone.

One day a village boy came up and asked, "Tell me, where did you come at this golden chain about your waist?"

The madman started—the chain that once was iron was verily gold; it was not a dream, but he did not know when it had changed.

He struck his forehead wildly—where, O where had he without knowing it achieved success?

It had grown into a habit, to pick up pebbles and touch the chain, and to throw them away without looking to see if a change had come; thus the madman found and lost the touchstone.

The sun was sinking low in the west, the sky was of gold.

The madman returned on his footsteps to seek anew the lost treasure, with his strength gone, his body bent, and his heart in the dust, like a tree uprooted.

67

Though the evening comes with slow steps and has signalled for all
    songs to cease;
Though your companions have gone to their rest and you are tired;
Though fear broods in the dark and the face of the sky is veiled;
Yet, bird, O my bird, listen to me, do not close your wings.

That is not the gloom of the leaves of the forest, that is the sea swelling
    like a dark black snake.
That is not the dance of the flowering jasmine, that is flashing foam.
Ah, where is the sunny green shore, where is your nest?
Bird, O my bird, listen to me, do not close your wings.

The lone night lies along your path, the dawn sleeps behind the
    shadowy hills.
The stars hold their breath counting the hours, the feeble moon swims
    the deep night.
Bird, O my bird, listen to me, do not close your wings.

There is no hope, no fear for you.
There is no word, no whisper, no cry.
There is no home, no bed for rest.
There is only your own pair of wings and the pathless sky.
Bird, O my bird, listen to me, do not close your wings.

None lives forever, brother, and nothing lasts for long. Keep that in
 mind and rejoice.
Our life is not the one old burden, our path is not the one long
 journey.
One sole poet has not to sing one aged song.
The flower fades and dies; but he who wears the flower has not to
 mourn for it forever.
Brother, keep that in mind and rejoice.

There must come a full pause to weave perfection into music.
Life droops toward its sunset to be drowned in the golden shadows.
Love must be called from its play to drink sorrow and be borne to the
 heaven of tears.
Brother, keep that in mind and rejoice.

We hasten to gather our flowers lest they are plundered by the passing
 winds.
It quickens our blood and brightens our eyes to snatch kisses that
 would vanish if we delayed.
Our life is eager, our desires are keen, for time tolls the bell of parting.
Brother, keep that in mind and rejoice.

There is not time for us to clasp a thing and crush it and fling it away
 to the dust.
The hours trip rapidly away, hiding their dreams in their skirts.
Our life is short; it yields but a few days for love.
Were it for work and drudgery it would be endlessly long.
Brother, keep that in mind and rejoice.

Beauty is sweet to us, because she dances to the same fleeting tune
 with our lives.
Knowledge is precious to us, because we shall never have time to
 complete it.
All is done and finished in the eternal Heaven.
But earth's flowers of illusion are kept eternally fresh by death.
Brother, keep that in mind and rejoice.

69

I hunt for the golden stag.

You may smile, my friends, but I pursue the vision that eludes me.

I run across hills and dales, I wander through nameless lands, because
    I am hunting for the golden stag.

You come and buy in the market and go back to your homes laden
    with goods, but the spell of the homeless winds has touched me I
    know not when and where.

I have no care in my heart; all my belongings I have left far behind me.

I run across hills and dales, I wander through nameless lands—
    because I am hunting for the golden stag.

I remember a day in my childhood I floated a paper boat in the ditch.
It was a wet day of July; I was alone and happy over my play.
I floated my paper boat in the ditch.

Suddenly the storm clouds thickened, winds came in gusts, and rain
poured in torrents.
Rills of muddy water rushed and swelled the stream and sunk my boat.
Bitterly I thought in my mind that the storm came on purpose to spoil
my happiness; all its malice was against me.

The cloudy day of July is long today, and I have been musing over all
those games in life wherein I was loser.
I was blaming my fate for the many tricks it played on me, when
suddenly I remembered the paper boat that sank in the ditch.

The day is not yet done, the fair is not over, the fair on the
    river-bank.
I had feared that my time had been squandered and my last
    penny lost.
But no, my brother, I have still something left. My fate has not
    cheated me of everything.

The selling and buying are over.
All the dues on both sides have been gathered in, and it is time for me
    to go home.
But, gatekeeper, do you ask for your toll?
Do not fear, I have still something left. My fate has not cheated me of
    everything.

The lull in the wind threatens storm, and the lowering clouds in the
    west bode no good.
The hushed water waits for the wind.
I hurry to cross the river before the night overtakes me.
O ferryman, you want your fee!
Yes, brother, I have still something left. My fate has not cheated me of
    everything.

In the wayside under the tree sits the beggar. Alas, he looks at my face
    with a timid hope!
He thinks I am rich with the day's profit.
Yes, brother, I have still something left. My fate has not cheated me of
    everything.

The night grows dark and the road lonely. Fireflies gleam among the
    leaves.
Who are you that follow me with stealthy silent steps?
Ah, I know, it is your desire to rob me of all my gains. I will not
    disappoint you!
For I still have something left, and my fate has not cheated me of
    everything.

At midnight I reach home. My hands are empty.

You are waiting with anxious eyes at my door, sleepless and silent.

Like a timorous bird you fly to my breast with eager love.

Ay, ay, my God, much remains still. My fate has not cheated me of everything.

With days of hard travail I raised a temple. It had no doors or
windows, its walls were thickly built with massive stones.
I forgot all else, I shunned all the world, I gazed in rapt contemplation
at the image I had set upon the altar.
It was always night inside, and lit by the lamps of perfumed oil.
The ceaseless smoke of incense wound my heart in its heavy coils.
Sleepless, I carved on the walls fantastic figures in mazy bewildering
lines—winged horses, flowers with human faces, women with
limbs like serpents.
No passage was left anywhere through which could enter the song of
birds, the murmur of leaves or hum of the busy village.
The only sound that echoed in its dark dome was that of incantations
which I chanted.
My mind became keen and still like a pointed flame, my senses
swooned in ecstasy.
I knew not how time passed till the thunderstone had struck the
temple, and a pain stung me through the heart.

The lamp looked pale and ashamed; the carvings on the walls, like
chained dreams, stared meaningless in the light as they would fain
hide themselves.
I looked at the image on the altar. I saw it smiling and alive with the
living touch of God. The night I had imprisoned had spread its
wings and vanished.

Infinite wealth is not yours, my patient and dusky mother dust!

You toil to fill the mouths of your children, but food is scarce.

The gift of gladness that you have for us is never perfect.

The toys that you make for your children are fragile.

You cannot satisfy all our hungry hopes, but should I desert you for
    that?

Your smile which is shadowed with pain is sweet to my eyes.

Your love which knows not fulfilment is dear to my heart.

From your breast you have fed us with life but not immortality, that is
    why your eyes are ever wakeful.

For ages you are working with colour and song, yet your heaven is not
    built, but only its sad suggestion.

Over your creations of beauty there is the mist of tears.

I will pour my songs into your mute heart, and my love into your love.

I will worship you with labour.

I have seen your tender face and I love your mournful dust, Mother
    Earth.

In the world's audience hall, the simple blade of grass sits on the same
    carpet with the sunbeam and the stars of midnight.
Thus my songs share their seats in the heart of the world with the
    music of the clouds and forests.
But, you man of riches, your wealth has no part in the simple grandeur
    of the sun's glad gold and the mellow gleam of the musing moon.
The blessing of all-embracing sky is not shed upon it.
And when death appears, it pales and withers and crumbles into dust.

At midnight the would-be ascetic announced:

"This is the time to give up my home and seek for God. Ah, who has
    held me so long in delusion here?"

God whispered, "I," but the ears of the man were stopped.

With a baby asleep at her breast lay his wife, peacefully sleeping on
    one side of the bed.

The man said, "Who are ye that have fooled me so long?"

The voice said again, "They are God," but he heard it not.

The baby cried out in its dream, nestling close to its mother.

God commanded, "Stop, fool, leave not thy home," but still he
    heard not.

God sighed and complained, "Why does my servant wander to seek
    me, forsaking me?"

The fair was on before the temple. It had rained from the early
morning and the day came to its end.

Brighter than all the gladness of the crowd was the bright smile of a
girl who bought for a farthing a whistle of palm leaf.

The shrill joy of that whistle floated above all laughter and noise.

An endless throng of people came and jostled together. The road was
muddy, the river in flood, the field under water in ceaseless rain.

Greater than all the troubles of the crowd was a little boy's trouble—
he had not a farthing to buy a painted stick.

His wistful eyes gazing at the shop made this whole meeting of men
so pitiful.

The workman and his wife from the west country are busy digging to
make bricks for the kiln.

Their little daughter goes to the landing-place by the river; there she
has no end of scouring and scrubbing of pots and pans.

Her little brother, with shaven head and brown, naked, mud- covered
limbs, follows after her and waits patiently on the high bank at her
bidding.

She goes back home with the full pitcher poised on her head, the
shining brass pot in her left hand, holding the child with her
right—she the tiny servant of her mother, grave with the weight of
the household cares.

One day I saw this naked boy sitting with legs outstretched.

In the water his sister sat rubbing a drinking-pot with a handful of
earth, turning it round and round.

Near by a soft-haired lamb stood gazing along the bank.

It came close to where the boy sat and suddenly bleated aloud, and the
child started up and screamed.

His sister left off cleaning her pot and ran up.

She took up her brother in one arm and the lamb in the other, and
dividing her caresses between them bound in one bond of affection
the offspring of beast and man.

It was in May. The sultry noon seemed endlessly long. The dry earth
    gaped with thirst in the heat.
When I heard from the riverside a voice calling, "Come, my darling!"
I shut my book and opened the window to look out.
I saw a big buffalo with mud-stained hide, standing near the river with
    placid, patient eyes; and a youth, knee deep in water, calling it to
    its bath.
I smiled amused and felt a touch of sweetness in my heart.

79

I often wonder where lie hidden the boundaries of recognition
between man and the beast whose heart knows no spoken
language.

Through what primal paradise in a remote morning of creation ran the
simple path by which their hearts visited each other.

Those marks of their constant tread have not been effaced though their
kinship has been long forgotten.

Yet suddenly in some wordless music the dim memory wakes up and
the beast gazes into the man's face with a tender trust, and the man
looks down into its eyes with amused affection.

It seems that the two friends meet masked and vaguely know each
other through the disguise.

With a glance of your eyes you could plunder all the wealth of songs
    struck from poets' harps, fair woman!
But for their praises you have no ear, therefore I come to praise you.
You could humble at your feet the proudest heads in the world.
But it is your loved ones, unknown to fame, whom you choose to
    worship, therefore I worship you.
The perfection of your arms would add glory to kingly splendour with
    their touch.
But you use them to sweep away the dust, and to make clean your
    humble home, therefore I am filled with awe.

Why do you whisper so faintly in my ears, O Death, my Death?
When the flowers droop in the evening and cattle come back to their
stalls, you stealthily come to my side and speak words that I do not
understand.
Is this how you must woo and win me with the opiate of drowsy
murmur and cold kisses, O Death, my Death?

Will there be no proud ceremony for our wedding?
Will you not tie up with a wreath your tawny coiled locks?
Is there none to carry your banner before you, and will not the night
be on fire with your red torch-lights, O Death, my Death?

Come with your conch-shells sounding, come in the sleepless night.
Dress me with a crimson mantle, grasp my hand and take me.
Let your chariot be ready at my door with your horses neighing
impatiently.
Raise my veil and look at my face proudly, O Death, my Death!

We are to play the game of death tonight, my bride and I.

The night is black, the clouds in the sky are capricious, and the waves
are raving at sea.

We have left our bed of dreams, flung open the door and come out,
my bride and I.

We sit upon a swing, and the storm winds give us a wild push from
behind.

My bride starts up with fear and delight, she trembles and clings to
my breast.

Long have I served her tenderly.

I made for her a bed of flowers and I closed the doors to shut out the
rude light from her eyes.

I kissed her gently on her lips and whispered softly in her ears till she
half swooned in languor.

She was lost in the endless mist of vague sweetness.

She answered not to my touch, my songs failed to arouse her.

Tonight has come to us the call of the storm from the wild.

My bride has shivered and stood up, she has clasped my hand and
come out.

Her hair is flying in the wind, her veil is fluttering, her garland rustles
over her breast.

The push of death has swung her into life.

We are face to face and heart to heart, my bride and I.

She dwelt on the hillside by the edge of a maize-field, near the spring that flows in laughing rills through the solemn shadows of ancient trees. The women came there to fill their jars, and travellers would sit there to rest and talk. She worked and dreamed daily to the tune of the bubbling stream.

One evening the stranger came down from the cloud-hidden peak; his locks were tangled like drowsy snakes. We asked in wonder, "Who are you?" He answered not but sat by the garrulous stream and silently gazed at the hut where she dwelt. Our hearts quaked in fear and we came back home when it was night.

Next morning when the women came to fetch water at the spring by the *deodar* trees, they found the doors open in her hut, but her voice was gone and where was her smiling face? The empty jar lay on the floor and her lamp had burnt itself out in the corner. No one knew where she had fled to before it was morning—and the stranger had gone.

In the month of May the sun grew strong and the snow melted, and we sat by the spring and wept. We wondered in our mind, "Is there a spring in the land where she has gone and where she can fill her vessel in these hot thirsty days?" And we asked each other in dismay, "Is there a land beyond these hills where we live?"

It was a summer night; the breeze blew from the south; and I sat in her deserted room where the lamp stood still unlit. When suddenly from before my eyes the hills vanished like curtains drawn aside. "Ah, it is she who comes. How are you, my child? Are you happy? But where can you shelter under this open sky? And, alas, our spring is not here to allay your thirst."

"Here is the same sky," she said, "only free from the fencing hills,—this is the same stream grown into a river,—the same earth widened into a plain." "Everything is here," I sighed, "only we are not." She smiled sadly and said, "You are in my heart." I woke up and heard the babbling of the stream and the rustling of the *deodars* at night.

Over the green and yellow rice-fields sweep the shadows of the
    autumn clouds followed by the swift chasing sun.
The bees forget to sip their honey; drunken with light they foolishly
    hover and hum.
The ducks in the islands of the river clamour in joy for mere nothing.
Let none go back home, brothers, this morning, let none go to work.
Let us take the blue sky by storm and plunder space as we run.
Laughter floats in the air like foam on the flood.
Brothers, let us squander our morning in futile songs.

85

Who are you, reader, reading my poems an hundred years hence?
I cannot send you one single flower from this wealth of the spring, one
   single streak of gold from yonder clouds.
Open your doors and look abroad.
From your blossoming garden gather fragrant memories of the
   vanished flowers of an hundred years before.
In the joy of your heart may you feel the living joy that sang one
   spring morning, sending its glad voice across an hundred years.

A Note About the Author

Rabindranath Tagore (1861–1941) was an Indian poet, composer, philosopher, and painter from Bengal. Born to a prominent Brahmo Samaj family, Tagore was raised mostly by servants following his mother's untimely death. His father, a leading philosopher and reformer, hosted countless artists and intellectuals at the family mansion in Calcutta, introducing his children to poets, philosophers, and musicians from a young age. Tagore avoided conventional education, instead reading voraciously and studying astronomy, science, Sanskrit, and classical Indian poetry. As a teenager, he began publishing poems and short stories in Bengali and Maithili. Following his father's wish for him to become a barrister, Tagore read law for a brief period at University College London, where he soon turned to studying the works of Shakespeare and Thomas Browne. In 1883, Tagore returned to India to marry and manage his ancestral estates. During this time, Tagore published his *Manasi* (1890) poems and met the folk poet Gagan Harkara, with whom he would work to compose popular songs. In 1901, having written countless poems, plays, and short stories, Tagore founded an ashram, but his work as a spiritual leader was tragically disrupted by the deaths of his wife and two of their children, followed by his father's death in 1905. In 1913, Tagore was awarded the Nobel Prize in Literature, making him the first lyricist and non-European to be awarded the distinction. Over the next several decades, Tagore wrote his influential novel *The Home and the World* (1916), toured dozens of countries, and advocated on behalf of Dalits and other oppressed peoples.

A Note from the Publisher

Spanning many genres, from non-fiction essays to literature classics to children's books and lyric poetry, Mint Edition books showcase the master works of our time in a modern new package. The text is freshly typeset, is clean and easy to read, and features a new note about the author in each volume. Many books also include exclusive new introductory material. Every book boasts a striking new cover, which makes it as appropriate for collecting as it is for gift giving. Mint Edition books are only printed when a reader orders them, so natural resources are not wasted. We're proud that our books are never manufactured in excess and exist only in the exact quantity they need to be read and enjoyed.

bookfinity™

Discover more of your favorite classics with Bookfinity™.

- Track your reading with custom book lists.
- Get great book recommendations for your personalized Reader Type.
- Add reviews for your favorite books.
- AND MUCH MORE!

Visit **bookfinity.com** and take the fun Reader Type quiz to get started.

Enjoy our classic and modern companion pairings!

Classic & Modern

www.ingramcontent.com/pod-product-compliance
Lightning Source LLC
Chambersburg PA
CBHW021135020426
42331CB00005B/778